STOCKH

Bryony Lavery

STOCKHOLM

methuen | drama

LONDON • NEW YORK • OXFORD • NEW DELHI • SYDNEY

METHUEN DRAMA
Bloomsbury Publishing Plc
50 Bedford Square, London, WC1B 3DP, UK
1385 Broadway, New York, NY 10018, USA
29 Earlsfort Terrace, Dublin 2, Ireland

BLOOMSBURY, METHUEN DRAMA and the Methuen Drama logo
are trademarks of Bloomsbury Publishing Plc

First published in Great Britain by Oberon Books 2007
This edition published by Methuen Drama 2021
Reprinted 2023

A catalogue record for this book is available from the British Library.

A catalog record for this book is available from the Library of Congress.

ISBN: PB: 978-1-3502-7536-2

Series: Modern Plays

Printed and bound in Great Britain

To find out more about our authors and books visit www.bloomsbury.com
and sign up for our newsletters.

Characters

TODD
KALI

A Frantic Assembly and Drum Theatre Plymouth Production in association with Brighton Festival and Hampstead Theatre. Stockholm was first performed on 21 September 2007 at the Drum Theatre Plymouth.

CAST

Kali **Georgina Lamb**
Todd **Samuel James**

CREATIVE TEAM

Writer **Bryony Lavery**
Direction and Choreography **Scott Graham and Steven Hoggett**
Design **Laura Hopkins**
Lighting Design **Andy Purves**
Sound Design **Adrienne Quartly**
Casting Director **Ginny Schiller**
Tango Choreography Consultant **Jack Murphy**

PRODUCTION TEAM

Production Manager **Nick Ferguson**
Company Stage Manager **Joni Carter**
Stage Manager **Nick Hill**
Production Electrician **Mark Jones**
Production Runner **Sarah Hopkins**

FOR DRUM THEATRE PLYMOUTH

Production Manager **David Miller**
Costume Supervisor **Lorna Price**
Sets, Props and Costumes **TR2 – Theatre Royal Plymouth Production Centre**

FOR FRANTIC ASSEMBLY

Producer **Lisa Maguire**
Creative Learning and Admin Manager **Laura Sutton**
Creative Learning Associate **Neil Bettles**
Marketing **Clair Chamberlain, The Corner Shop PR**
Press **Ben Chamberlain, The Corner Shop PR**
Photography **Richard Haughton**
Graphic Design **John Pasche** www.johnpasche.com

Developed at the National Theatre Studio

Frantic Assembly would like to thank: Amanda Lawrence, Ben Wright, Bryan Dick, Daniel Evans, Delphine Gaborit, Geir Hytten, Lynsey Turner and Martin Holbraad. David Sibley, John Tiffany, Steve Kirkham and Sue Kyd. Mary Teasdale, Michael Camp, Sandro Martini, Sian Graham, William Graham. Cue One and 3 Mills Studios.

A free resource pack for Stockholm is available to download from www.franticassembly.co.uk. The website also contains information on a special programme of workshops and teachers INSETs to accompany Stockholm and details of forthcoming training sessions open to all.

ARTISTIC DIRECTORS' NOTES

Stockholm was inspired by a real event, namely witnessing people we cared about destroy each other and not being able to intervene. That position of impotence and frustration lives long in the memory.

In this production we did not want to judge the protagonists. We wanted to get inside their relationship and get an understanding of what they mean by love and what makes them run back to each other. We have always talked about Stockholm as a love story that simply requires a wider definition of love. It is uncomfortable, difficult and traumatic but as soon as we started talking about this idea to others it was remarkable how many people talked so eloquently about their experiences within such relationships. What really stood out was people's complete commitment to the relationship at the time. It was only when they eventually emerged outside the relationship that they found some perspective.

This led us to research Stockholm Syndrome and its fascinating bond between perceived victim and aggressor. This relationship is incomprehensible from the outside but perfectly clear from within and seemed to be born from the same climate of fear and potential violence. Stockholm Syndrome seemed to be the world we wanted to explore.

Designer Laura Hopkins has made this world real and more. She has delivered a set that provides the perfect contrast between domestic bliss and intrinsic danger. Lighting Designer Andy Purves and Sound Designer Adrienne Quartly are currently offering us new and exciting ways to make this world both fantastical and terrifying.

Sam and George are two remarkable performers. Their sensitive performance instincts are as brave and impressive as their awesome physicality. This is a fairly intense subject matter and, being a two hander, the work is relentless and there is nowhere to hide. They keep coming back for more and have been a joy to work with.

And in Bryony we have found an incredible collaborator. It has been a thrilling process grappling with her unique mind. Every stage of development has felt like we are inspiring and bringing the best out of each other and we are already planning our next collaboration.

9 April 2008

We are on our way to meet Bryony to talk to her about another project we want to work with her on. After Stockholm and It Snows (for National Theatre Connections), working with Bryony could easily become an addiction. Both of the previous projects were such invigorating joys that we just want more, more, more.

But first we have the opportunity to bring Stockholm back. After an incredibly successful tour it is so exciting to be able to present this show again, to see Sam and George's stunning performances in front of new audiences. We believe very strongly in the power of this production and hope you enjoy watching it as much as we enjoyed making it. Otherwise, we are in trouble...

REHEARSAL POST-IT NOTES BETWEEN TODD AND KALI

I'LL BE THINKING ABOUT YOU ALL DAY T x

order paint.

I'VE BOUGHT YOU SOMETHING. BE WEARING IT WHEN I GET HOME.

You are MY Infinity xx

I'M SORRY T x

Washing up?!!

You Fucker.

WE NEED TO TALK ABOUT LAST NIGHT

♡ x

Look in the drawer under the bed.

HEY Sexy, SHALL WE GO OUT FOR DINNER TONIGHT?

always. X

Fuck me now

SURPRISE!! x

V. Sexy.

LAST NIGHT WAS SO FUCKING HOT ...... THAT'LL GET ME THRU 2DAY.

Stockholm Music Tracks and Inspirations

Stockholm Music
_____

BT - This Binary Universe
  Monster

Cinematic Orchestra - Ma Fleur

Yann Tiersen - Goodbye Lenin

John Powell - The Italian Job

John Hopkins - Opalescent

Simon Bottle - Perfume

Evelyne Glennie

Ebb

Aphex Twin

Jazz Kammer

Jaga Jazzist

David Julyen - Memento

Seu George Jorge
Leonard Cohen
Sweet Billy Pilgrim
4 Hero
Laurie Anderson
Gonzalez

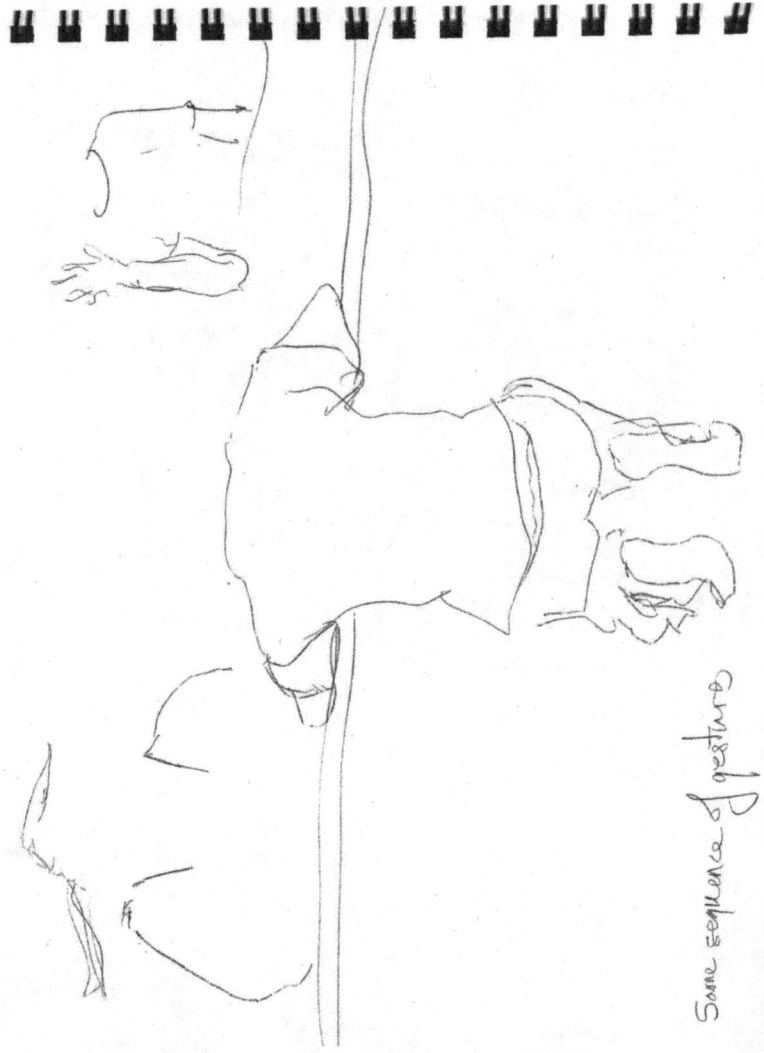

Some sequence of gestures

Stockholm 1/5

Does Stock. Syn. require 3 parties:-

OPPRESSOR ———— OPPRESSED

SOCIETY / LAW

∨

• Feets w/ task - putting on jumper }
            putting on watch }
            hair pomzle
            video camera - put tape in

Create a warm trace of some disco routine)
two of you made up together. Top 1/2 only

Put in room - Kitchen - pedestrianise it as
well as be functional up top.

FROM BRYONY LAVERY'S NOTEBOOK

We are outside.
Lovely spring weather.
TODD is there. Off-kilter.
He has shopping.

TODD
It's
Saturday
In a few days   soon   they'll be in Stockholm.
They've both cleared their schedules.
Booked a *great* room.
Flights. They're flying 'Finn Air'   **He grins**
Everything's been planned with 'Mission Impossible *One*'
close-attention-to-detail brilliance…
It's going to be Magic.
He can't wait.
That cold bright city.
Magnetically pulling him…

He's a compass a weathervane a magnet he can find…

North.

Where   in summer   the sun shines all the time
Where   come winter   it's dark most of the most of the

But
That's in the future
This afternoon
They're returning hand in hand to the lovely home
They've made together…

And yet

It's quite weird…
He's lost her
He can't see her
And he wants to tell her something that just happened that
Look!

Spring arrived!

A sense of **[Sings]** 'Here comes the sun…'
A presence of   unopened buds
Warm wind gently blowing on his cheek
And   it's *unsettling* him…but not in a 'bud' way
Kali!
Where are you?

And KALI's there…
With identical shopping

KALI
Where were you?

TODD
Here.
Where were you?

KALI
There.   Newsagent.
Why didn't you come in with me?

TODD
Didn't see you go in.

Look!

KALI
I can't look.

TODD
It's Spring!!!

KALI
I'm still in the film

TODD
They're coming back from seeing a film
Wind…listen!

KALI
I can only hear Swedish

I love that film love it love it love it to death love it!

TODD
A matinee
They love going to films together in the afternoon

KALI
Particularly when it's *Someone's* Birthday!

TODD
Particularly then…as part of a spectacularly put-together
Birthday Day…

KALI
Afternoon. Film.
No Dick-flicks no Chick-flicks allowed.

TODD
Class.

KALI
Der seligen Sele

TODD
[**Prompts…**] subtitles…

KALI
The Seventh Seal.
I love Ingmar Bergman.
Fuck off Ingmar Bergman you were so fucking talented
Love him love him love him to death whoops! love him.

TODD
The Seventh Seal. A classic film.
A benchmark in Swedish…nay European nay World cinema…
They've been doing the late Bergman's entire oeuvre…

KALI
*Persona   Wild Strawberries   Summer with Monika   Silence…/
Fanny and Alexander…*now *The Seventh Seal…*

TODD
They're a thorough couple.

Hey…they want to be up to speed for Stockholm

KALI
Okay.
I want to be Swedish.

TODD
You can be Swedish when we go to Stockholm.

KALI
I want to be Swedish *now.*

TODD
Okay.   Uppen Lampen Moben Chairer Billy Bookcase…

KALI
That's not Swedish! That's *Ikean*…?

TODD
It's a Swedish *dialect*. From the *region* of Ikea…

KALI
Speak Swedish Chef dialect…

TODD
From the Swedish Chef region?
Okay. [SWEDISH CHEF – **something very dirty…**]
Herdleberdlishmerdli…?

KALI
[DITTO…**shocked**] Herdliberdlishmerdi?   Skadoo!

And she laughs with delight.

TODD
He likes to make her laugh
He loves to have her laughing
She's got an award-winning laugh…

[**Something even dirtier…**] Kenergen shmergen nergen

KALI
Nergen????

TODD
**[Something along the lines of 'I don't know what's
wrong with suggesting a good *nergen*']**
…Shnerdlibode nurdleshmerdle nergen

They are dancing back through the celluloid Swedish
countryside
They are a susceptible and imaginative twosome…
Everywhere threatened with The Black Death
Everyone else in comedy tights
They are hoping that *they are* the lovely couple who escape
The Plague

KALI
And they are…

TODD
And   they're home.

With their key
He lets them in
Welcome to their house.

TWO – INTERIOR: OUR GLORIOUS HOME

KALI
This place   when they first saw it…

TODD
Two years ago   only two years ago!

**They put down their identical shopping and…
They go
Back in time…**

KALI
Come in here. Take a look.

TODD
She brings me into this amazing place…

And they are there…

He shudders...

KALI
What?

TODD
Nothing.
Wow.

KALI
'Wow' *exactement!*

TODD
Back then, she wanted to be *French...*

KALI
Went off French.

TODD
Aujourd'hui, elle déteste France, *Grand Style...*

KALI
The place.

TODD
The place

KALI
Fucking empty echoing nightmare

TODD
Nothing but a pleassic-jurassic sofa amid the quietly looming
mildewed debris...

KALI
Which they   with Proustian precision   shagged on

TODD
Their christening

KALI
Made it theirs   sort of *Rosemary's Baby...*

Seizing their fate…

Bought it
Took it
gutted it

TODD
Pleassic-jurassic sofa…

Impressive mime of them both throwing the sofa strong as super-heroes *The Incredibles* into the far cosmos…

KALI
Took it back to just the four walls really
They got an architect friend of theirs

TODD
Mick
My old friend who became her new friend

KALI
who drew up
The most wonderful plans
They've worked like slaves
But it was worth it

TODD
So worth it

They repick up their identical shopping…

KALI
It's got   no scintilla of irony   the *wow* factor

TODD
Shnerdlibo wow!

KALI
It's exactly how they wanted it
Look at it
Look at it
It was worth it   all the…   all of it

THREE – A DARK HALL WITH A MOTH IN IT

They put their identical shopping down in...

KALI
This is their surprisingly-large-for-this-style-property-hall.

TODD
Postman's been.

On the retro ironic 'welcome' mat...

There's a letter.

She looks.

KALI
It's for you.

Ooh.

From 'Mummy'

A terrible embarrassing outpouring of longing from the letter inside the envelope...

MUMMY
...Todd!   Todd!
TODDYYYYYY!!! Oh, Todd darling darling darling Todd
Todd Todd Toddy...what are you doing where've you gone
why've you gone oh oh oh Todd Todd my boy!!!!

TODD
Fuck!
Shut the fuck *up*!
What *is* this...fucking *'Mommie Dearest'?????*

KALI
Is he going to open *that* envelope of worms?

TODD
Leave it there.
Not *that!*

MUMMY
Todd! Toddy!!!! Mummy wants you! Mummy wants you back!!! Todd!!!

TODD
[To the letter inside the envelope]

Not on my Birthday!!!!

To her…

I'm not going to let that mad bitch ruin our day!

KALI
My Good Boy.

My Wannabe Orphan.

Luckily, we don't read English…we're Swedish

ShmerdliberdliAFuck?

TODD
No not just

KALI
We're Swedish
I'm Swedish
You're Swedish…
ShmerdliberdliAFuck?

TODD
Skadoo   **['no']**

KALI
Skadoo
Skadoo, A Fuck?
Hmmm…
Well then…
ShmerdliberdiaSuck?

TODD
Skadoo

KALI

Skadoo?

Don't 'skadoo' me
Never 'skadoo' me
Don't give me that old 'skadoo'
Don't be skadoogative with *me!*
I won't take 'skadoo' for an answer

And she pins him against the wall as...

TODD

And he leans back against the paint of the wall of the hall
Of the house that Love built
In the hall they decorated together
And let's her take unzip him
Detrouser him
Peel his outer layer
Her onion

**She performs an accomplished and elegant sex act upon
him as**

That's 'Harlequin *Indulgence*' **[the wallpaper]**
That's '*Rich Praline*' **[the paintwork]**

It was dark it was so depressingly dark in here
It needed some light
It needed some natural light...

Look at the floor.
These tiles...
This colour gives a rugged warmth to the...doesn't it?
These tiles are from an architectural salvage supply company
They picked them out individually from a pile in the yard
Arranged them into their own pattern...
They're really really really old
But God aren't they *beautiful...?*

And   she   pleasures   is that what you say in your
language?   him
His Swedish Film Star
Except...

While it's happening
There's a   fluttering   off left
Around near   his head
A   something alive   a not of him…

He tries to watch it…

It   with wings   lands

On the letter from his fucking mother

And

He can see

It's a moth!!!

Something in like charcoal on its furry head

Is it A skull…?

a moth in their dark hall

And he is…

I don't think I can

She holds him in his last throes as…

He's not alone he's not alone he's not alone he's not alone
He's not alone he's not alone he's not alone he's not alone
He's not alone he's not alone   **[until…]**
He's   *Alone!!!!*

And he's come.

KALI
I love you.

TODD
I love you.

KALI
That'll be 50 krone, please.
You Swedish fucker.

**And it's all laughter and light…and wild dancing…
impossibly over walls and ceilings…**

TODD
He can't wait to go to Stockholm.

FOUR – A CUPBOARD UNDER THE STAIRS

She picks up the identical shopping...

She gets past
He looks at the letter from his mother.
Something grips him

US
Don't touch it!
We've got something else for you to do...
Lay your hands upon a large servicable bag that can hold
Everything
Fill it with happiness
Complete utter radiant eternal happiness.
That's the plan.
Nothing has to go wrong
Nothing
It's got to be
Perfect.
A big bag of happiness.
It's not much to ask.
Get it.

And it pushes him back out of the confined space, out of the cupboard.
KALI is somewhere unpacking the shopping

KALI
[Off] Where are you?

TODD
Here

KALI
[Off] What's wrong?

TODD
Nothing.

Coming.

FIVE – A BLOWN-UP PHOTOGRAPH – OUR FIRST MEAL

She is in their beautiful knocked-through kitchen-living space...
Shopping unpacked on a surface...now...
She takes out a couple of bottles of champagne.

KALI
This is their unique selling point knocked-through-kitchen-cum-living space

They don't drink much usually.
Don't need to.
They are naturally filled with intoxication!
But tonight...she's got him a lovely surprise...
His favourite...
La Veuve...
The Widow!

She hides it.   Ready for later. Ready.

She opens a fridge.
Something insides receives, with ecstasy, the champagne...

US
Yes Yes Yes
Yes Yes
Yesssssss!!!!

She closes the fridge.
TODD enters the kitchen space.

They unpack and sort the shopping brilliantly.
They show us that they could unpack shopping for England.

Olympic Standard Unpack Team.

There's a photo framed right next to the fridge…

KALI
This is them
The night they met
When they became *us*
Just a Polaroid someone took but
she said 'let me have that…'
Had it touched up
Blown up kerboom to this…
She was at a restaurant opening
A restaurant that's closed now
She's taking you for a brief moment a visit back in time

And she whisks us back to…

She's a hell of a time witch
Big night
Restaurant opening under new improved management
There was a taster menu…
She can't remember who else was there…?
Hadn't she come with friends?
She can't have come alone
That's not *her*…
And who was *he* with…?
Doesn't matter
It doesn't matter
It doesn't matter…
Who was *he* with?
Who?
Who?
Who?
Stop.
Doesn't…
She must ask him
Who *he* came with…
That blonde girl…
She must ask him……

What did we talk about…?
She can't remember them even speaking…
Some music was playing
The music was
The music was

And it is playing…

And all she can see take in is…

The near aspect

The near aspect is a table, two knives, two forks, glasses…

Stranger enters

He comes in…

And   for a moment   there's absolutely nothing about this ordinary
him that would…

TODD
Hi

Adam

KALI
Hi

Eve

TODD
No!!!

KALI
Actually…No.

TODD
Actually…no either.
Actually…David.

KALI
Hi David.

Victoria…

They are sitting down opposite one another…

TODD
No!

KALI
Actually No!!!

TODD
Actually…again   No!

Actually…Bond. James Bond.

KALI
Actually, any one of those fucking vacuous male fantasy
fucking plastic cunt holes just for fucking in any of those
fucking dick flicks…
let's settle for
                    Pussy

TODD
He likes her intensity

KALI
She likes that he likes her intensity
It's something she's been working on
Although   actually   it's really not something she needs to
work on…
Shall we start again?

TODD
Todd.

KALI
Nice name.   Foxy.
Kali.

TODD
Nice name too.
Sort of

They look at one another.

Food arrived at some point…

They start to drink one another
They start to cut each other up and eat each other…
And pour each other and drink each other
They savour and devour each other
during which…

TODD
Delicious.

It's like   something in the food that night in the drink
That night

KALI
Like the menu read…

Lotus Fruit   come to my island
or

That fucking flower out of *Midsummer Night's Dream* that goes
on the lids makes the eyes… **[droop]**

Rohypnol

TODD
He's never tasted anything quite like it before.

It makes him forget things

Oh   what…?

KALI
She's experienced this before   where?

Who?

Not *this* intense

Not this   *delicious*

And back in the Now…

From that moment?

Inseparable

The Siamese Twins

Where are you?

TODD
Here

Can we have some music on please?

KALI
Music. Sure.   Yes.

And there is music...

He's looking out of their window

Towards the distant horizon
Except
There is no view of the distant horizon from this room...

What is he looking for?

She watches him looking out

She's got to make sure he enjoys his birthday...

He must be given a lovely day

She starts to dance with him...
It goes everywhere dangerous...

No going in the fridge.
There's a big surprise in there.
You must apply to me in writing if you want to go in the fridge..
Okay?

TODD
I'm cooking...how the/...hell?

KALI

To Me. In Writing.

TODD
Okay.

SIX – AND YET ANOTHER ONE LAST DANCE...

TODD
[As he dances]

I absolutely cannot dance with you now.
I have to think about our supper.

And she says

KALI
Please.

One last dance.

TODD
Look at the time!
I have to cook su/...

KALI
/The club's closing
The music.........................they'll turn it off after this one
This last dance oh!
It's a slow one
And there's just the two of them
Out on the dance floor
And

TODD
We love each others to bits

KALI
You're my world
You are my night and day

TODD
Swirling

He is an epilectic under a glitter ball

KALI
Everybody's moved back to watch them

Ooooooh!!!

TODD

Every time…every time they dance together…
A serried global gasp of awful awe

BOTH

Aaaaaaah!!!

KALI

Turning

We're dancing
We're in each other's arms
We're holding each other close
We're in step
We're part of the music   oh!
We *are* the music
They're playing…
It's our song!!!
And we dance
And we dance
And we dance
And we dance
And   who was the blonde girl you were in the restaurant
with
That time?

TODD

What time… [**He knows 'what' time?**]

KALI

That first time.
Our first meeting
Sweetheart
That blonde thing
With the sagging great mango tits…

TODD

Repeat after me.

She was called Josette…

BOTH

She was called Josette.
She was French.
She now lives in Marseilles with a very nice doctor
And two adorable French children
And has no plans   we believe   for reconnecting with Todd
Pour une rencontre avec Todd

TODD

He's losing all his fucking French now he doesn't speak it any more…
And we've been through this.
What did we agree?
What did we agree?

BOTH

We agreed that retro-jealousy
Over past lovers was a waste of cosmic time…

Dumb

Stupid

KALI

That we trust one another
That our love is strong   impenetrable
can
Move mountains
Ford rivers
Survive three months of Serbian builders

TODD

Dearest darling beautiful wonderful thing
Do you know how much I love adore lust love fantasise want
need have to have must have love passionately eternally
perpetually love you desire you want you?

They look at one another

US

No sorry. Not good enough. If this is the best you can do…
Just not good enough. We're gonna have to call it a day. End
of. Period.

KALI

Don't leave me.

TODD

I won't leave you.

Their landline rings

SEVEN – HAPPY BIRTHDAY FROM YOUR CRAZY FAMILY

KALI

Do you want to get that?

TODD

No.

This is hallowed holy sacred 'us' time.

Do you want to get it?

KALI

She can't bear phones.
She's probably phone-phobic that's probably…
Available you're so fucking available these days…
Fucking phones.

**Ansaphone clicks. Their recorded comedy-message.
It records them trying out their new music/sound
effect-making software package…they aspire to Laurie
Anderson's 'O Superman'.
Quite new, it amuses them…**

TODD / KALI

Hello, this is Us.   Us us us us usssssssssss
KALI… Me.
TODD… and Me.
KALI… Kaaaaaaaali……

TODD... Toddoddoddoddodd
BOTH... Why Are You Calling Us At A Time Like This???
Why are you calling us at a time like this????
TODD... If you must *absolutely* must
KALI... and only then...
TODD... leave a short message which we probably
Won't respond to...
Otherwise
BOTH... JUST   FUCK   OFF

Into song...

FUCK OFF
FUCK OFF

TODD
God, we're Good!

Ansaphone clicks in...

ANSAPHONE
Hello, it's Mummy.
Just ringing to send love to you both...
Hello...Kali...dear
And, of course, Happy Birthday, Todd Darling!
We don't know what you're doing today...
You might be in Stockholm already...
I can't remember when you're going...
Anyway...whatever you're doing...
I hope you're having a wonderful time...
And so does Daddy...

Pause
Then...

MOTHER / FATHER
[Almost in tune...]

Happy Birthday to you
Happy Birthday to you
Happy birthday dear To-odd...
Happy Birthday to you!

MOTHER
Happy Birthday, darling!

FATHER
Yes. Happy Birthday, er…Happy Birthday, son.

Pause…

MOTHER
[Background…]
Hang up now, for goodness sake Frank, please, quick, we're not…hang…

Clicks off

KALI
How sweet.

Mummy and Daddy.

Mummy *and* Daddy.

Calling on your Big Day, Little Boy.

Why didn't you pick up?

TODD
Cooking to do.

Honestly, people making me *dance*
Wanting me to *talk* to them…

KALI
Don't you want to talk to them?

TODD
Not at this moment in time, no.

KALI
But you *do* want to talk to them *some* moment in time.

On your birthday…

Don't you.

Don't you?

TODD
Well, they *are* my parents!

Later

BOTH
See

No

KALI
You do want to talk to them really.

Oh yes.

They are your family, after all.

Even if she is Cunt of Cunt Hall.

Lady Cunt.

And Lord Cunt-Fuck too.

Lord and Lady Cunt-Fuck of Cunt-Fuck Manor…

Your *parents* after all   …even *despite* their Cunt-Fuck Manor treatment of *me*

Call them

Call them

It's your birthday

Call them

TODD
No.

No.

KALI
Why won't you call them?

Why?

Why?

TODD
I   DO   NOT   WANT   TO.

KALI

Why not? Why not?

Because…?

TODD

Because I can't stand my parents for fuck sake!

Because I hate how they treat you!

Because I want to be with just *you* on my birthday.

Because I want to cook our dream dinner now.

Can I please cook our dream dinner now?

KALI

Do what you like.

I've stuff to do upstairs.

TODD

What stuff?

KALI

Private stuff.

TODD

What private stuff?

KALI

Private private stuff.

Can I borrow your mobile?

TODD

Why d'you want to borrow my mobile?

KALI

I just do.

TODD

Is yours broken?

KALI

No. Is yours?

TODD
No.

KALI
Well, then, let me borrow it. Mardy-arse.
Please. Thank you.

And she gets it...

And now he can't just call or speak or text or email
Because she knows he won't dare use the landline and she's
got this and she's going on the computer so all he can do is
sneak out the door...

TODD
[Calls up...]

I'm just popping down to the shop!

KALI
See?

Why?

TODD
We forgot fennel!

KALI
Do without fennel.

TODD
It'll only take a minute!

KALI
Do without fucking fennel.

TODD
But it's good with fish...

KALI
We don't need fennel.

TODD
But with fish it's...

KALI
Can we seriously not live without fennel?

TODD
Yes, but…

A lot of silence in both their spaces…
Oh.

Alright. We can live without fennel.

KALI
Why does he want to leave such a lovely house…?

Why does he pretend to forget the fennel?
So he can sneak out to pretend he's buying fucking fennel?

How remedial does he think she is?

EIGHT – FISH

He stares at the ingredients.

TODD
No fucking fennel.   Fennelless. Sans la fenouille. Skadoo
Fennel.

Okay.

Potatoes.

Rosemary. That's for Remembrance.

Strawberries. Chocolate. That's for Hot Sex.

Mixed leaves. That's for Roughage.

He opens the fish. Lays out two trout staring up at him.

Don't look at me like that.

You old trout.

He takes a fuck-off knife out of a block.
**Some fabulous 'Pirates-of-the-Caribbean' cutlass work
with it as…**

NINE – THE ATTIC OF STARS

She's in the office attic...

KALI

This attic might be her favourite room

It was just roof space   far as the eye can

Full of junk

All the families who used to live here just dumped all their shit up here...magazines newspapers from Biblical times old photographs she's not a Big Fan of 'Families'

There was a desiccated fossilised flat mouse stuck to this floor joist just here

Where she's standing now...just a model city of piles piles piles of shit
some baby clothes filthy rolls of early wallpaper with a garish but now faded space rocket design...

Nearly *filled* the largest size skip!

Fucking families

They've made it so they can stand up straight in it

They've put in velux windows   so they can see for miles upon city miles

God, the views

This is the one room in the house they can see to the distant horizon...

But she doesn't look at that...

Who has he been phoning?

She investigates his mobile

Who has he been texting?

Mick

Mick

Topher

Work

Work

Mick

Mummy   Lady Cunt-Fuck has learned how to text...
Interesting...

Nothing in his calls
Ansaphone empty.

No shit Sherlock!

Let's go into missed calls...elementary my dear Watson...

Missed calls...

Topher Mick   *Domino Pizza!* Mr Gordon-fucking-Ramsay???
Mick

Hello?

A number she doesn't recognise...
But has been expecting...

A Mystery number

She calls the mystery number

Ansaphone message   woman's voice...

She's called Louise...

She wants me to leave a message...

No chance, Cunt!

So

She was right

A leopard does not change his   acne

US
Look all you like
Look as far as you like
You're still earthbound Earthling
These are not your stars
There are no stars for you
You cannot see constellations

You're a blind girl
You're a deaf girl
You have learning difficulties
You are mind impaired
Nowhere you look is far enough away for you
You are a black hole
You are an infinite black hole
We are very disappointed to discover you still do not
Realise this!

And they give her back...
shuts the mobile

Yes...from this room...the most fabulous views...
You can see Iceland on a clear day...

She's looking out of the window...

At night, stars. Fuck   the stars you can see.

And   for her last Christmas...
He always buys her extravagant presents
...he bought her *a telescope!!!*

She puts her hand on it.

He's shown her and shown her how to use the fucking thing...
But every time she tries to do it on her own...
It fucking fucks up

She looks through
Nothing!

Gives it a vicious shake...

It's a sort of library reference officey space

The desk   here   with all the bose and mac-ery and
ipoddery...
Makes it like the flight deck of the Starship Enterprise...
Like she's the controller of something...

but mostly
up here
she wishes he had given her

an instrument that hasn't been invented yet...
something small enough to conceal

something so powerful
it can look into someone's brain
and see what they are thinking...
to know absolutely
that someone means what he says...

What are you doing?

TODD
[From downstairs...]
Cooking

What are you doing?

KALI
Reading

And she looks at something on the screen...

TEN – A FISH RECIPE

And in their separate spaces...
TODD goes near to the landline phone.
Looks at it for a bit...goes back to...

TODD
'in a pan gently sweat...the onions, leeks, garlic and *fennel*...'

KALI
'Quality Hotel Prince Olaf
Oxholmsgrand 2
Stockholm
Sweden
Come to this charming hotel
consisting of just 32 rooms all equipped to ensure a
comfortable stay for our guests and leave all your everyday
cares at home'...

TODD
'gently sweat hah!…in butter just to start the softening
process…'
all the vegetables…
softening process…

**He somehow discovers himself by the landline receiver
again.**

He goes to the fridge

KALI
'each "premium" rate room possesses a luxurious
private bathroom with a top-of-the-range array of comfort
products to soak all those cares away…'

'Massages are available inquire at reception professionally-
trained Swedish hands will make those tensions disappear…'

**He discovers he is singing something incriminating…like
'I just called to say I love you…' he stops.**

'Extensive mini-bar.

Private wet room

Trouser press…'

**He opens the fridge.
He finds the champagne.**

**He looks at it.
Puts it back.
He shuts the fridge.
Goes back to reading the recipe…**

TODD
'Gently sweat in butter
…Just to start the softening process but not so that they give
up all resistance…'

KALI
'Thoroughly relaxed
it is now time to visit the Local attractions

which include the Folk Museum,   the world's largest IKEA store…'

TODD
'Season'

TODD's mobile goes
KALI answers it…

KALI
His mobile goes

TODD
His mobile goes

KALI
Hello?

TODD
He hopes it's not…

He listens intently…

KALI
Topher!

Good!

Actually, he's in the middle of cooking…/you know what he's like when he's *cooking*!

You can talk to me though…tell me…

Oh, I'm sure he'd have loved that! You should have given us more notice we've made plans for toni…

Home

Romantic Dinner For Two

Aw shame

Where are you all going?

Aw. Shame.

Yeah   I'll tell him.

We would have loved that!

TODD
'Lay the vegetables as a bed for your fish.'

Make your bed.

'Place your fish on its vegetable bed.'

Then lie on it

'Dot
With knobs of butter '

You knob.

KALI
[**Quieter…**] Hey, Topher…
Do you know anybody called Louise?

TODD
'Check the fish with a knife..'

Gutted.

KALI
No…somebody left a message

[**It's very light, unimportant…**] and
we've no fucking idea who she is!

TODD
'the flesh should fall easily off the bone'

KALI
It's probably a wrong number then.

Yeah. Stockholm.

Departing London Heathrow 16.25
Arriving Arlanda Stockholm 19.55

We're flying Finn Air   [**She laughs**]

Can't wait.

Oh! I can smell food. Got to go…

Yeah

We'll send you a postcard of The Largest IKEA store in the Universe. Bye

ELEVEN – WHO'S LOUISE?

She descends, hands him back his mobile

KALI
Thanks

TODD
Oh   Thank you

Finished with it?

KALI
Completely

Topher says 'Happy Birthday'

TODD
That's it?

'Happy Birthday'?

No 'Your Harley Davidson 850 Vintage Edition with Sidecar is on its way?'

KALI
Oh, yeah. He said that was on its way.

TODD
I should fucking think so!

KALI
He was talking about some girl. Louise. Do you know her?

She's watching him, everything for clues...

TODD
Don't think so. No.

KALI
Well.

She looks at the deeply-amusing clock they bought together at The Conran Sale...

Look! Seven o'clock!

Time for...

She opens the fridge...

KALI
Happy Birthday!

She has two champagne bottles

TODD
Do we need that?

Weren't we going to go teetotal till...

KALI
It's your birthday!

Stockholm soon!

He watches her open a bottle.
Pour champagne.
Hand him a glass.

To Stockholm!

TODD
To Stockholm!

They drink.
He slowly.
She drains the glass.
Pours another.

KALI
Drink up.

TODD
I will.

I'm cooking.

And he is, in the dangerous kitchen…
KALI drinks champagne, watches him cook…as

KALI
Here's to Us!

TODD
Here's to Us!

TWELVE – THE FLIGHT DETAILS TO STOCKHOLM

KALI
Birthday Dance Time

TODD
Not yet

KALI
Yes

TODD
I'm cooking

KALI
Cook *afterwards*

TODD
Cook first
afterwards
afterwards

and they dance a bit, he really wants to cook…

KALI
Best meal…ever?

TODD
This one

KALI
You are gorgeous
Not counting this one.

TODD
I can't think.
Let's just cook
I'm cooking.
Cook with me.
Chop something.

KALI
Go on.

Best meal ever.

TODD
Well not really a meal…but…
Our second fuck…
The champagne strawberry chocolate ice cubes cigarette thing
We got into in the hotel room with the uneven floor…

KALI
that was good
that was hot
how hot was that?

Best meal ever.
Not counting anything we've had together.
Best meal ever…*before*

TODD
ooohhh…

KALI
It's in there…
I can see it
I've got this invisible gismo for seeing into your brain…
Yep
Look!
lovely memory…get it out…on the table…

TODD
Okay.
grilled fresh tomatoes
fabulous dressing…fresh herbs loads of them

some weird pink wine
then
grilled sardines…great plateful of them…
then   just cheese   some soft like goat cheese…

Pause

KALI
Where was this

TODD
France.

South of France.

KALI
South of France where?

TODD
Just   a little town called something like…Grenn…ulle…or
olle or something

KALI
When was this?

TODD
Oh. *Years* ago.

I was a *student* for fuck's sake!

Camping

KALI
This was with…?

TODD
Oh, just this other student.

Pause.

Er. Nickie.   That was it. Nickie.

KALI
Not 'Josette'?

TODD
No!

KALI
Not twitty fair-hair mango tits?

TODD
No…

KALI
This was   a   girlfriend?

TODD
Er…sort of… Very casual…I mean   real kid's stuff…I mean…
college!

KALI
But you were sleeping together?

TODD
Well   yes
What did we agree about retro/-jealousy?

KALI
Oh this isn't retro-jealousy
This is contempt this is disgust this is about fundamental
unchangeable character you slept with her but it was just
casual?

TODD
Let's not do this it's my/…

KALI
Look at your face
Look at your smug face
With your delicious French meal
And your 'Er…Nickie I think', 'Yeah…Nick! Nickie!'
Knickers!
And a leopard never changes its student-acne-spots does it
We can still slope off for a delicious meal fuck meal fuck
Meal fuck cunt mobile cunt mobile/ cunt mobile

TODD
What are you talking about...?

KALI
Your smug fucking gorgeous face.

TODD
And
Incredibly rapidly
She claws his face

KALI
Don't lie to me.

TODD
I'm not.

KALI
And this time
Her hand whole arm like a mare kicking lashes out

TODD
He sees for a few seconds galaxies of stars

KALI
Liar.

Lying.

Porkies.

Mendacity.

TODD
Please.

For once.

Let's not do this.

It's my birthday.

KALI
You can't lie to me.

Liar.

Lies

Who's Louise?

TODD
Louise?

I don't know a Louise

There isn't a fucking Louise

KALI
Oh but there is.

Oh but there is.

It's phenomenonally difficult to catch you out you clever
fucking CuntFuck Manor Boy
But I've caught you out at last…

TODD
This again?

KALI
Let's remove that smug fucking expression…

And now, a terrible beautiful fight.

Let's kill him for this betrayal

**She, trying for his absolute annihilation.
He, trying to hold her, contain her until the fury passes.
But, it's probably a beautiful wild dance…**

TODD
This
With improvisations on a theme
Is how its goes
She leaps for him

KALI
You *fucker!!!!*

**He hits her.
She ricochets**

KALI

Right.

Good.

He hit her.

Get the police.

Domestic violence.

He's going down.

Where's her phone?

Where's her fucking phone?????

THIRTEEN – THE TIME IN STOCKHOLM

He takes the clock off the wall.
Shows it to her.

TODD

whose is this clock?
your clock?
my clock?
our clock?
well, guess what…

Smashes its face into a hard surface.
Shows it to her…

See the time?

this is the exact time
this thing is over
the time this ends!

He puts the clock down.

He dis-arms

Do what you like.

Anything.

Kill

Murder

Destroy

Finish it.

He offers himself to her.

I'm too intelligent for this

This is stupid

This is stupid behaviour

This makes us stupid

He hands her his mobile.

Here.   Use mine.

Call someone.

Call anyone.

She does not take up his offer.
He goes back to cooking.
She watches him.
Occasionally, she tries to offer things... Herbs? A utensil?
He ignores it. Or not.
He is indifferent.

When she feels it absolutely...
then
absolute remorse.

KALI
Let's get help.

He just carries on clearing up.

I'll get help

I'll see somebody.

I'm too intelligent for this too.

He just carries on clearing.

I know it's me

She sits and watches him...

TODD
[As he tidies...]
It's like getting to the summit of the medium-difficult climb
the violence   then the after   is the best bit
because he doesn't have to read her
stop her
control her
because she *is* going to do it
and all the rest is leading up to it
gentle incline
or steep slope
always leading up to the same top of the same hill with the
same view

it's actually relief   the violence

he won't feel the parrot scratches wont start to smart till later
her bites usually really start to nip I mean really 'ouch'
after about twenty minutes
her playful punching of the six-pack she is so proud of calls
forth a pain similar only to an uber-tough exercise regime
the occasional lucky bone dislocation or break usually a finger
usually a little or third finger
mends surprisingly quickly...

And now she really is...

KALI
I'm sorry

She truly is. Does she cry?
They both sit.
He watches her for a bit
When he feels, *really* feels forgiveness, true forgiveness...
Then he goes over to her

TODD
There is simply no way of telling anyone outside of this
How attractive it is   true remorse

Because it *is* real
She feels it from the bottom of her heart…

**He wraps his arms round her
She climbs into him**

FOURTEEN – BEDWORLD

He picks her up and they go to a dangerous bed as…

BOTH
We're not sure this isn't our favourite part of the situation!

TODD
Because   what is delightful   is that   at this moment
We actually think it is going to be different from now on!

KALI
What is *delicious* is that we actually *believe* we'll get out of the
situation…

TODD
Actually believe in all the press coverage!
'Hostages saved!
Hostages recovered without physical harm!'

KALI
'the helicopters circling the squads of cops in kevlar vests the
strategy just went in surrounded the innocent hostages and
pulled them out of there!'

TODD
Let's have a little sleep

KALI
Us little hostages are given…

A little late nap

TODD
But what's best about it is

The little present we give each other

The sweetener

The treat

For forgiving each other

They are on the bed...
And very tender wonderful love-making...as...

The terrific terrific terrific warm loving we have

KALI
When we feel the war's over

TODD
The absolute heaven absolute bliss we have

KALI
When we are allies   victorious allies
Succeeding against all the odds...

TODD
When we are completely *us*

They fall asleep.
They throw their sleeping shapes in their pattern.
Even in their sleep, there is territory, negotiation and
danger.
Once, only once during the whole thing, they are both
awake at the same time. At this moment, they look at
each other

Eyes close
The shapes continue

As they sleep...

FIFTEEN – A DARK AND DINGY CELLAR

A terrible dark hole opens somewhere...
And they are in...

US
this is the cellar

a coldness to it no sun could warm
if any sun ever reached down here

a smell of mildew mould   rat droppings
old human blood
in this space in this space
there's too little space
they can't stand upright
can't stretch
no far horizon

here's where we discover our hostages

He and she lie, affectionate, sleepy…
There is just a radiator. They are chained to it.

TODD
We should get started on the cellar soon

KALI
I know
We'll do it as soon as we get back from Stockholm…

US
Yes
Eventually
In the future
Sometime
later
They'll find in this cellar
Look
Squashed flat on the cement floor
Their children
who they know won't be breathing
will be still as dolls
smothered
cotdeathed
these are the children these two   make   grow up
beauties beautiful children with their

fragile   easy-bruising snap-happy limbs
the children who make the newspaper story
when he walks out
when he walks out for good this time
and she calls him   on his mobile
and says 'If you don't come back   I can't go on living'
and she puts their eldest child on the phone
says   'tell Daddy'
'tell Daddy you want to go where Mummy's going'
and the eldest child says
'I love you Daddy. Please come back.'
And he's impotent with rage at the poor sentimental dialogue
She's been made to memorise his eldest daughter
These are the children in the car in the lay-by
These are the ones who drink the Ribena with the sleeping
pills crushed up in it
These are the ones she gets to phone him all that long last
night...
As the car fills   not with air

TODD
Strip it right back

Gut it absolutely

KALI
Yes.

Okay.

Good.

As soon as we get back from Stockholm.

And they rise
Ascend to their kitchen...
There are voices from the outside all the way up...

MUMMY
Are you alright, Todd?
Why don't you drop in? Just for a coffee or something...
Bring   Kali...both of you be lovely to see both of you...

TOPHER
Mate.
Topher.
Call me.
Fucking call me.
You never call me.

MICK
Todd! It's Mick. You there? I've sourced those tiles…
You want to swing by and see them?
Any time.
Be nice to see you.
I never see you.

LOUISE
Hello, this is Louise…
Todd…
Could you call me back.
It's urgent.

But he ignores them all

SIXTEEN – IN THE BRIGHT NIGHTKITCHEN

They both cradle in their hands mugs of warm, odourful steaming hot chocolate…

KALI
it's been a lovely day

they woke up entwined like orang-utans in each others' arms

TODD
they had a late breakfast out

KALI
That nice new place… 'Coffee'

TODD
they sat outside
the coffee smelled like a door opening

early spring

KALI
but it felt like summer

TODD
But it felt like summer

KALI
a blessed day

TODD
they sat in a dark cinema
saw a piece of great cinematic art
he   popcorn
she

KALI
… a small bag of Maltesers

they shared happily

They had one of their rows!

They're both very strong individual characters…

TODD
Almost at the end of the day
She discovered that the name of the travel agent they booked
their Stockholm stuff with is called…

KALI
Louise

TODD
To tell them they've been upgraded.
You pillock.

KALI
I am. I'm a pillock.

They smile at one another.

TODD
there was a plentiful amount of really rather splendid sex

BOTH
They have Olympic Golds in that category.

KALI
he cooked

they ate

TODD
Even without fennel...
The meal was a triumph

KALI
they danced

TODD
in a few days' time
they will have a holiday

Stockholm.